PAN STEEL DRUMS MADE EASY

Basics for Beginners

By
Harry Best

- Steel Drum/Pan de-mystified in four easy sessions
- 12 exercises for complete control
- Begin playing tunes immediately

Contents

Layout: Circle of Fifths   Orientation: Traditional

Pan Preface

This book was written primarily as a supportive tool for students enrolled in the PanWest instruction program. As we are always open and alert to better ways of learning and playing pan, we are not resistant to adopting or proposing positive change. It is in this spirit that we present the following discussion.

While a standard way of tuning the lead pan has been accepted by most steel pan builders and players, we propose to add a new wrinkle to the ongoing debate on 'standardization'. Respecting what is admittedly accepted by the vast majority on this issue—the 'hanging' of the pan—we venture to solicit support for a small change.

The generally accepted way the pan hangs on its stand presents the lowest note 'C' at the six o'clock position **(Style B)**.

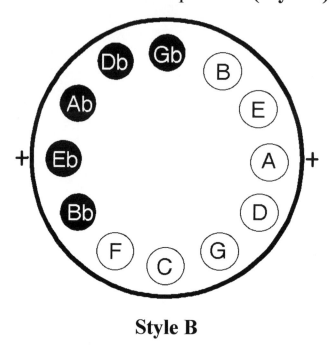

Style B

An **UpRight** setup with 'D' at the six o'clock position is what we propose as a better alternative **(Style A)**.

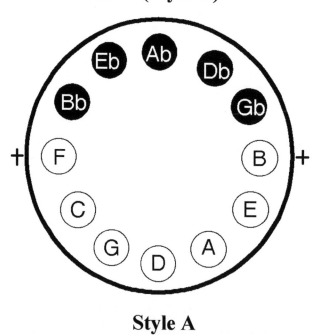

Style A

The advantage may seem merely graphic and perhaps trivial. But there are noteworthy advantages to this proposition. For one, it works far better for those playing from a music sheet. Secondly, the majority of songs seem to fall in the keys that relegate those playing pans in **Style B** to the right side of the pan. The **UpRight** position, **Style A**, finds one playing those same keys in a more evenly balanced position on the lower half of the pan.

If we consider the notes in the key of 'C' (C, D, E, F, G, A, B, C) to be the white/natural notes as in the case of a piano, and the accidentals (C#, D#, F#, G#, A#) to be the black/chromatic notes then Style B is skewed. However with the **UpRight** position, **Style A**, the pan is visually and practically balanced.

Of course, there are those who will argue that it really doesn't matter since, with the cycle of fifths, all scales follow the same pattern, so what note or key is at the navel position is irrelevant. Granted, but what is the rationale for having the 'C' at the six o'clock position? None. It is simply arbitrary. With that, we have adopted the **UpRight** position, **Style A** as our standard position. However, recognizing that we are in the minority for now, we will accommodate both styles.

You have the option of choosing from two editions of this instruction booklet: **Style A** for pans hanging **UpRight**, or **Style B** for pans hung in the **Traditional** manner.

Introduction

At **PanWest**, before you can begin classes, you must go through an obligatory interview with the instructor. The purpose of the interview is to lay the emotional groundwork that will motivate and inspire you throughout the course. This is arguably the most important session in the course.

The main reason for our overnight success with the **PanWest** instruction course is our holistic approach to learning. We approach our subject on three levels: emotional/spiritual, intellectual/mental, and physiological/material.

The first and most important step is to identify that mental picture that sparks your desire to begin to play pan or to improve. Depending on whether you have played pan before or you are a beginner, the questions might go like this:

1. Have you ever played pan? (If no, go to #4)
2. (If yes) Are you currently a pan player? (If yes, go to #5)
3. (If no) Why did you stop playing?
4. What made you decide to play pan, or to start again?
5. What do you hope to accomplish as a pan player?
6. What do you hope to accomplish on pan by the end of this course to consider it successful?
7. Are you willing to do what it takes to accomplish your goals?

That goal or expectation is the emotional and motivational seed that will bear fruit by the end of the course. In order to indelibly impress that picture on your psyche, you are lead in a short relaxation and visualization exercise that goes like this:

Sit comfortably, take a deep breath and begin to relax. As you breathe deeply concentrate on the different parts of your body starting from your toes and moving up slowly to the top of your head. When your body is completely relaxed, begin to quiet your thoughts. Focusing on your breath helps. With your eyes still closed, imagine a blank screen in front of you. On that screen begin to see yourself in action playing pan with the passion and fervor you always desired. Feel the emotion of the moment. Add color, sound and warmth to your picture. Include an audience if you desire. Make it a perfect picture of what you want to accomplish. Remember this picture, and keep it with you as a talisman. It will carry you through the doubtful periods.

Now that the emotional aspect is established, a modicum of music theory and some insights into the makeup of the instrument is all that is necessary, and will be provided, to add light and satisfy the intellectual/mental requirements.

The simple drills with sticks and pan will condition the physical/body to be able to deliver what you have conceived. If you then practice diligently, you can be confident of accomplishing your goal.

Session One

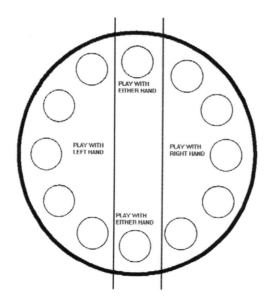

Layout

The layout of the 'cycle of fifths' pan is very symmetrical and makes for even dedication of left and right hands. Aim for equal work distribution of both hands.

Sticks/Mallets

The sticks or mallets for the lead pan are 6 to 8 inches long and should serve as an extension of the hand. Hold the stick between the thumb and index finger with the third finger at the bottom of the stick acting as a trigger.

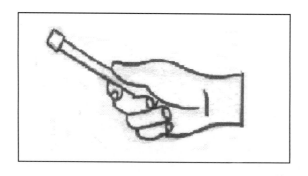

Allow the sticks to bounce off the notes. The smaller notes are much firmer and require a tighter grip when sticking. To sustain the sound of any note, roll evenly on the note alternating both sticks with wrist movement.

Mallet Control

Since the steel pan is a percussion instrument, rudimentary exercises for your hands to develop mallet control are fundamental. Each week, practice a progressively more challenging exercise. Do all drills with a metronome or rhythm machine whenever possible. Begin with the timer at 60. First practice the exercise in eighth notes, and finally in sixteenth notes. When you can comfortably maintain repetition with sixteenth notes for 30 seconds or more, you have mastered that particular drill. From here on, gradually increase the speed of your metronome.

Mallet Drill #1

Homework:
Practice **Mallet Drill #1** according to instructions given in the section on **Mallet Control.**

Session Two

Refresh

Begin each week's session by refreshing your motivating picture. This is more important than you might imagine. Sit down, relax and repeat the visualization process. It will help keep you focused and motivated.

Chromatic Scale

The chromatic scale is essential for learning the range (lowest to highest notes) and placement of notes on your pan. The scale is comprised of twelve consecutive tones each a half step apart.

When the chromatic scale is played ascending, the accidental notes (black notes) are called sharps. When the scale is played descending, these same notes are called flats.

When two notations refer to the same tone, they are called enharmonic. For example, C# and Db are two different names for the same tone. Thus they are called enharmonic.

Here is the scale and the sticking patterns for the **Traditional** hanging style **(B).** The first five notes are outlined and establish the pattern. With a little study it will become obvious. The note in the inner circle with the square inscribed is the octave:

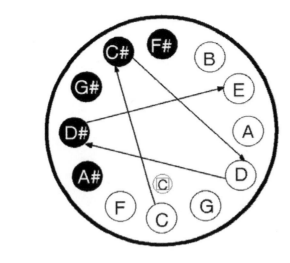

Ascending:	C	C#	D	D#	E	F	F#	G	G#	A	A#	B	C
Style B:	R	L	R	L	R	L	R	L	R	L	R	R	R

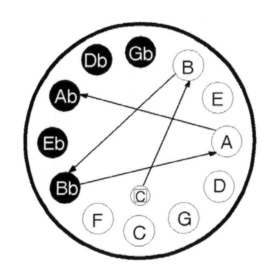

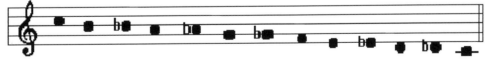

Descending:	C	B	Bb	A	Ab	G	Gb	F	E	Eb	D	Db	C
Style B:	R	R	L	R	L	R	L	L	R	L	R	L	R

11

Homework

1. Practice **Mallet Drill #2** according to instructions given in the section on **Mallet Control.**

2. Practice the Chromatic Scale (with metronome at 60), ascending and descending, first in eighths and in just one octave. A good idea is to take just four notes at a time. When you feel comfortable, add another set of four and in time the final four until you can play the entire 12-note scale with no interruption. About mid-week, extend the exercise to the second octave and increase your pace to sixteenth notes. By the end of the week you should have progressed to playing the entire chromatic scale, two octaves, ascending and descending in sixteenth beats.

NB: Pay attention to and begin to memorize the letter name and position of each note on your pan.

Session Three

Refresh

Do not be so eager to proceed with this lesson that you overlook the need to refresh your motivating picture. This is the time to tweak it, or make changes.

The Major Scale

The Major Scale pattern on the pan is easily learned once you understand that it is comprised of **two connected tetrachords that have the same movement pattern.** In other words, the first four notes of the Major scale (called a tetrachord), has the same movement pattern as the last four notes (another tetrachord). The following illustrations make this clear:

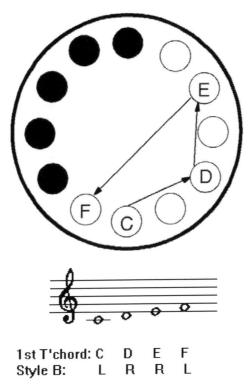

1st T'chord: C   D   E   F
Style B: L   R   R   L

Play the C note. Then skip one note (G) and play the D note. Skip the next note (A) and play the E note. Now cross over and play the F note. That's your **first tetrachord**.

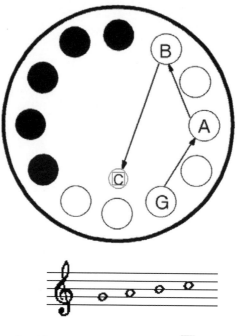

2nd T'chord: G   A   B   C
Style B: L   R   R   L

Continuing, skip the C note and play the G note. Then skip the D and play the A note. Skip the E and play the B note. Complete the **second tetrachord** by crossing over to the 'c' octave (small 'c'). You have just played the **C Major Scale.**

On your pan, the movement patterns of all 12 keys/Major scales are the same.

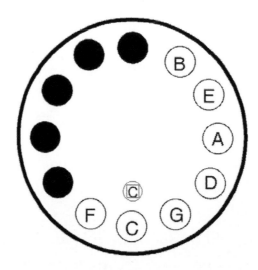

```
C major scale:  C   D   E   F   G   A   B   C
Style B:            L   R   R   L   L   R   R   L
```

Homework

1. Practice **Mallet Drill #3** according to instructions given in the section on **Mallet Control.**

Mallet Drill #3

```
R L R R   R L R R   R L R R   R

L R L L   L R L L   L R L L   L
```

2. Practice the C Major Scale (with metronome at 60) ascending and descending in eighth beats, and at first, in just one octave. As you feel more comfortable, extend your practice to the second octave and increase your tempo to sixteenth beats.

3. Begin to play and memorize the first two tunes in the Appendix: 'Mary Had a Little Lamb' and 'Twinkle Little Star'.

Refresh

The process of relaxing and refreshing your motivational picture before the start of each lesson is a valuable practice. It creates a conditioned response in your body making you more receptive to the new information.

Chords

Chords are derived from scales. They are constructed by using **alternate notes of the major scale.**

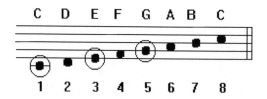

When the notes are played together it is called a chord; when played separately, it is called a chord arpeggio.

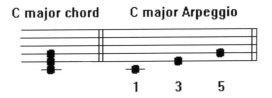

In the C Major scale there are two Major chords; one built on the C note (CEG) and the other on the F note (FAC).

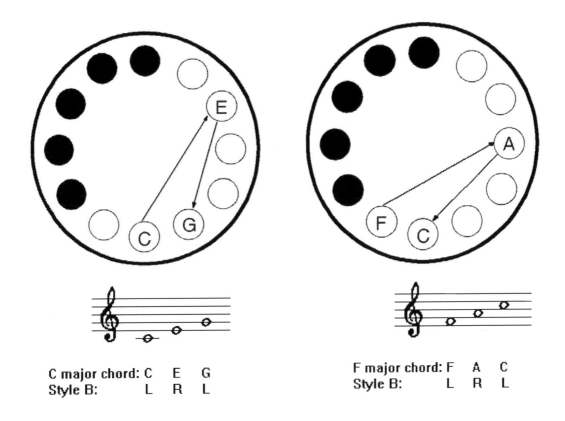

C major chord: C   E   G
Style B: L   R   L

F major chord: F   A   C
Style B: L   R   L

The minor chord is formed by lowering, by one half step, the middle note (the one which corresponds to the "3") of the Major chord with the same root. There are three minor chords in the C Major Scale. They are built on the D note (DFA), the A note (ACE) and the E note (EGB).

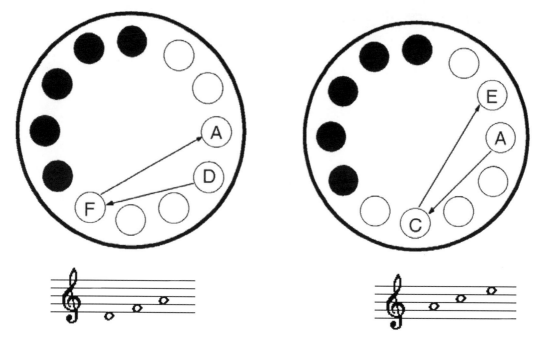

D minor chord: D   F   A
Style B: R   L   R

A minor chord: A   C   E
Style B: R   L   R

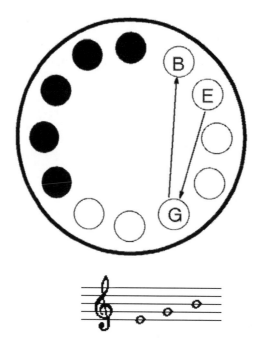

E minor chord: E   G   B
Style B: R   L   R

A Dominant Chord is a major chord with **an added minor 7th note**. This chord is usually built on the 5th note of the Major Scale. In the C Major Scale, that note is G (GBDF).

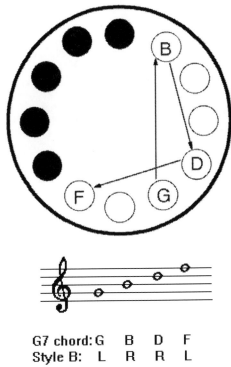

G7 chord: G   B   D   F
Style B: L   R   R   L

The Chord built on the B note (BDF) of the C Major Scale is called a **half-diminished chord.**

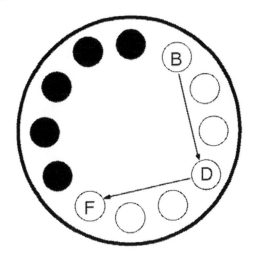

B♭ chord: B   D   F
Style B: R   R   L

Homework

1. Practice **Mallet Drill #4** according to instructions given in the section on **Mallet Control**.

R R R L   R R R L   R R R L   R

L L L R   L L L R   L L L R   L

2. With your metronome at 60, practice the seven chords in the C Major Scale, first in eighth beats and then in sixteenths. Here's an example of the exercise on the C Major Chord.

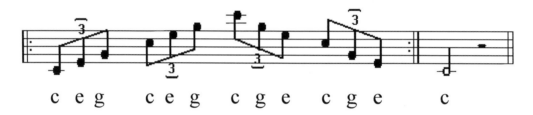

c e g   c e g   c g e   c g e   c

3. Play and memorize the next two tunes in the **Appendix**:

C Major

C Major scale (Up and Down)

C (L)	D (R)	E (R)	F (L)
G (L)	A (R)	B (R)	C (L)

C Major Thirds (Together and Separately)

C,E (LR)	D,F (RL)	E,G (RL)	F,A (LR)
G,B (LR)	A,C (RL)	B,D (RL)	C,E (LR)

C Major Triads (Up the Scale)

C,E,G (LRL)	D,F,A (RLR)	E,G,B (RLR)	F,A,C (LRL)
G,B,D (LRR)	A,C,E (RLR)	B,D,F (RRL)	C,E,G (LRL)

C Major Triads (Down the Scale)

G,E,C (LRL)	F,D,B (LRR)	E,C,A (RLR)	D,B,G (RRL)
C,A,F (LRL)	B,G,E (RLR)	A,F,D (RLR)	C (L)

C# Major

C# Major scale (Up and Down)

C#	D#/Eb	F	F#
(L)	(L/R)	(R)	(L)
G#	**A#/Bb**	**C**	**C#**
(L)	(R)	(R)	(L)

C# Major Thirds (Together and Separately)

C#,F	Eb,F#	F,G#	F#,Bb
(LR)	(RL)	(RL)	(LR)
G#,C	**Bb,C#**	**C,Eb**	**C#,F**
(LR)	(RL)	(RL)	(LR)

C# Major Triads (Up the Scale)

C#,F,G#	Eb,F#,Bb	F,G#,C	F#,Bb,C#
(LRL)	(RLR)	(RLR)	(LRL)
G#,C,Eb	**Bb,C#,F**	**C,Eb,F#**	**C#,F,G#**
(LRL)	(RLR)	(RRL)	(LRL)

C# Major Triads (Down the Scale)

G#,F,C#	F#,Eb,C	F,C#,Bb	Eb,C,G#
(LRL)	(LRR)	(RLR)	(RRL)
C#,Bb,F#	**C,G#,F**	**Bb,F#,Eb**	**C#**
(LRL)	(RLR)	(RLR)	(L)

D Major

D Major scale (Up and Down)

D	E	F#	G
(R)	(L)	(L)	(R)
A	B	C#	D
(R)	(L)	(L)	(R)

D Major Thirds (Together and Separately)

D,F#	E,G	F#,A	G,B
(RL)	(RR)	(LR)	(RL)
A,C#	B,D	C#,E	D,F#
(RL)	(LR)	(LR)	(RL)

D Major Triads (Up the Scale)

D,F#,A	E,G,B	F#,A,C#	G,B,D
(RLR)	(RRL)	(LRL)	(RLR)
A,C#,E	B,D,F#	C#,E,G	D,F#,A
(RLR)	(LRL)	(LRR)	RLRL)

D Major Triads (Down the Scale)

A,F#,D	G,E,C#	F#,D,B	E,C#,A
(RLR)	(RRL)	(LRL)	(RLR)
D,B,G	C#,A,F#	B,G,E	D
(RLR)	(LRL)	(LRR)	(R)

Eb Major

Eb Major scale (Up and Down)

Eb	F	G	Ab/G#
(L)	(R)	(R)	(L)
Bb	**C**	**D**	**Eb**
(L)	(R)	(R)	(L)

Eb Major Thirds (Together and Separately)

Eb,G	F,Ab/G#	G,Bb	G#,F
(LR)	(RL)	(RL)	(LR)
Bb,D	**C,Eb**	**D,F**	**Eb,G**
(LR)	(RL)	(RL)	(LR)

Eb Major Triads (Up the Scale)

Eb,G,Bb	F,Ab,C	G,Bb,D	G#,C,Eb
(LRL)	(RLR)	(RLR)	(LRL)
Bb,D,F	**C,Eb,G**	**D,F,G#**	**Eb,G,Bb**
(LRR)	(RLR)	(RRL)	(LRL)

Eb Major Triads (Down the Scale)

Bb,G,Eb	G#,F,D	G,Eb,C	F,D,Bb
(LRL)	(LRR)	(RLR)	(RRL)
Eb,C,G#	**D,Bb,G**	**C,G#,F**	**Eb**
(LRL)	(RLR)	(RLR)	(L)

E Major

E Major scale (Up and Down)

E	F#	G#	A
(R)	(L/R)	(L)	(R)
B	**C#**	**D#/Eb**	**F**
(R)	(L)	(L)	(R)

E Major Thirds (Together and Separately)

E,G#	F#,A	G#,B	A,C#
(RL)	(LR)	(LR)	(RL)
B,Eb	**C#,E**	**Eb,F#**	**E,G#**
(RL)	(LR)	(LR)	(RL)

E Major Triads (Up the Scale)

E,G#,B	F#,A,C#	G#,B,Eb	A,C#,E
(RLR)	(LRL)	(LRL)	(RLR)
B,Eb,F#	**C#,E,G#**	**Eb,F#,A**	**E,G#,B**
(RLR)	(LRL)	(LRR)	(RLR)

E Major Triads (Down the Scale)

B,G#,E	A,F#,Eb	G#,E,C#	F#,Eb,B
(RLR)	(RRL)	(LRL)	(RLR)
E,C#,A	**Eb,B,G#**	**C#,A,F#**	**E**
(RLR)	(LRL)	(LRL)	(L)

F Major

F Major scale (Up and Down)

F	G	A	Bb
(L)	(R)	(R)	(L)
C	D	E	F
(L)	(R)	(R)	(L)

F Major Thirds (Together and Separately)

F,A	G,Bb	A,C	Bb,D
(LR)	(RL)	(RL)	(LR)
C,E	D,F	E,G	F,A
(LR)	(RL)	(RL)	(LR)

F Major Triads (Up the Scale)

F,A,C	G,Bb,D	A,C,E	Bb,D,F
(LRL)	(RLR)	(RLR)	(LRL)
C,E,G	D,F,A	E,G,Bb	F,A,C
(LRR)	(RLR)	(RRL)	(LRL)

F Major Triads (Down the Scale)

C,A,F	Bb,G,E	A,F,D	G,E,C
(LRL)	(LRR)	(RLR)	(RRL)
F,D,Bb	E,C,A	D,Bb,G	F
(LRL)	(RLR)	(RLR)	(L)

F# Major

F# Major scale (Up and Down)

F# (R)	G# (L)	A#/Bb (L)	B (R)
C# (R)	D#/Eb (L)	F (L)	F# (R)

F# Major Thirds (Together and Separately)

F#,Bb (RL)	G#,B (LR)	Bb,C# (LR)	B,Eb (RL)
C#,F (RL)	Eb,F# (LR)	F,G# (LR)	F#,Bb (RL)

F# Major Triads (Up the Scale)

F#,Bb,C# (RLR)	G#,B,Eb (LRL)	Bb,C#,F (LRL)	B,Eb,F# (RLR)
C#,F,G# (RLR)	Eb,F#,Bb (LRL)	F,G#B (LRR)	F#,Bb,C# (RLR)

F# Major Triads (Down the Scale)

C#,Bb,F# (RLR)	B,G#,F (RLL)	Bb,F#,Eb (LRL)	G#,F,C# (LLR)
F#,Eb,B (RLR)	F,C#,Bb (LRL)	Eb,B,G# (LRL)	F# (R)

G Major

G Major scale (Up and Down)

G	A	B	C
(R)	(L)	(L)	(R)
D	**E**	**F#**	**G**
(R)	(L)	(L)	(R)

G Major Thirds (Together and Separately)

G,B	A,C	B,D	C,E
(RL)	(RL)	(LR)	(RL)
D,F#	**E,G**	**F#,A**	**G,B**
(RL)	(LR)	(LR)	(RL)

G Major Triads (Up the Scale)

G,B,D	A,C,E	B,D,F#	C,E,G
(RLR)	(LRL)	(LRL)	(RLR)
D,F#,A	**E,G,B**	**F#,A,C**	**G,B,D**
(RLR)	(LRL)	(LRR)	(RLR)

G Major Triads (Down the Scale)

D,B,G	C,A,F#	B,G,E	A,F#,D
(RLR)	(RLL)	(LRL)	(LLR)
G,E,C	**F#,D,B**	**E,C,A**	**G**
(RLR)	(LRL)	(LRL)	(R)

G# Major

G# Major scale (Up and Down)

G#	Bb	C	C#
(L)	(R)	(R)	(L)
Eb	F	G	G#
(L)	(R)	(R)	(L)

G# Major Thirds (Together and Separately)

G#,C	Bb,C#	C,Eb	C#,F
(LR)	(RL)	(RL)	(LR)
Eb,G	F,G#	G,Bb	G#,C
(LR)	(RL)	(RL)	(LR)

G# Major Triads (Up the Scale)

G#,C,Eb	Bb,C#,F	C,Eb,G	C#,F,G#
(LRL)	(RLR)	(RLR)	(LRL)
Eb,G,Bb	F,G#,C	G,Bb,C#	G#,C,Eb
(LRL)	(RLR)	(RRL)	(LRL)

G# Major Triads (Down the Scale)

Eb,C,G#	C#,Bb,G	C,G#,F	Bb,G,Eb
(LRL)	(LRR)	(RLR)	(RRL)
G#,F,C#	G,Eb,C	F,C#,Bb	G#
(LRL)	(RLR)	(RLR)	(L)

A Major

A Major scale (Up and Down)

A	B	C#	D
(R)	(L)	(L)	(R)
E	F#	G#	A
(R)	(L)	(L)	(R)

A Major Thirds (Together and Separately)

A,C#	B,D	C#,E	D,F#
(RL)	(LR)	(LR)	(RL)
E,G#	F#,A	G#,B	A,C#
(RL)	(LR)	(LR)	(RL)

A Major Triads (Up the Scale)

A,C#,E	B,D,F#	C#,E,G#	D,F#,A
(RLR)	(LRL)	(LRL)	(RLR)
E,G#,B	F#,A,C#	G#,B,D	A,C#,E
(RLR)	(LRL)	(LRR)	(RLR)

A Major Triads (Down the Scale)

E,C#,A	D,B,G#	C#,A,F#	B,G#,E
(RLR)	(RRL)	(LRL)	(RLR)
A,F#,D	G#,E,C#	F#,D,B	A
(RLR)	(LRL)	(LRR)	(R)

Bb Major

Bb Major scale (Up and Down)

Bb	C	D	Eb
(L)	(R)	(R)	(L)
F	G	A	Bb
(L)	(R)	(R)	(L)

Bb Major Thirds (Together and Separately)

Bb,D	C,Eb	D,F,	Eb,G
(LR)	(RL)	(RL)	(LR)
F,A	G,Bb	A,C	Bb,D
(LR)	(RL)	(RL)	(LR)

Bb Major Triads (Up the Scale)

Bb,D,F	C,Eb,G	D,F,A	Eb,G,Bb
(LRL)	(RLR)	(RLR)	(LRL)
F,A,C	G,Bb,D	A,C,Eb	Bb,D,F
(LRR)	(RLR)	(RRL)	(LRL)

Bb Major Triads (Down the Scale)

F,D,Bb	Eb,C,A	D,Bb,G	C,A,F
(LRL)	(LRR)	(RLR)	(RRL)
Bb,G,Eb	A,F,D	G,Eb,C	Bb
(LRL)	(RLR)	(RLR)	(L)

B Major

B Major scale (Up and Down)

B	C#	Eb	E
(R)	(L)	(L)	(R)
F#	**G#**	**Bb**	**B**
(R)	(L)	(L)	(R)

B Major Thirds (Together and Separately)

B,Eb	C#,E	Eb,F#	E,G#
(RL)	(LR)	(LR)	(RL)
F#,Bb	**G#,B**	**Bb,C#**	**B,Eb**
(RL)	(LR)	(LL)	(RL)

B Major Triads (Up the Scale)

B,Eb,F#	C#,E,G#	Eb,F#,Bb	E,G#,B
(RLR)	(LRL)	(LRL)	(RLR)
F#,Bb,C#	**G#,B,Eb**	**Bb,C#,E**	**B,Eb,F#**
(RLL)	(LRL)	(LLR)	(RLR)

B Major Triads (Down the Scale)

F#,Eb,B	E,G#,Bb	Eb,B,Ab	C#,Bb,F#
(RLR)	(RLL)	(LRL)	(LLR)
B,G#,E	**Bb,F#,Eb**	**G#,E,C#**	**B**
(RLR)	(LRL)	(LRL)	(R)

Appendix

Simple Melodies

(MARY HAD A LITTLE LAMB)

(TWINKLE, TWINKLE LITTLE STAR)

(LONDON BRIDGE)

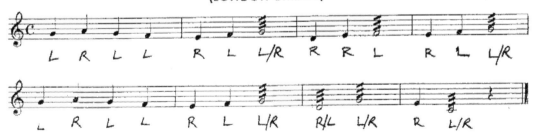

(FRÈRE JACQUES)

(AIR)

MOZART

(YANKEE DOODLE)

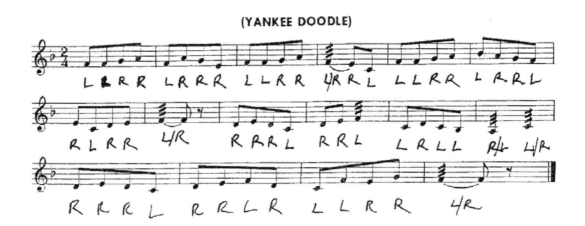

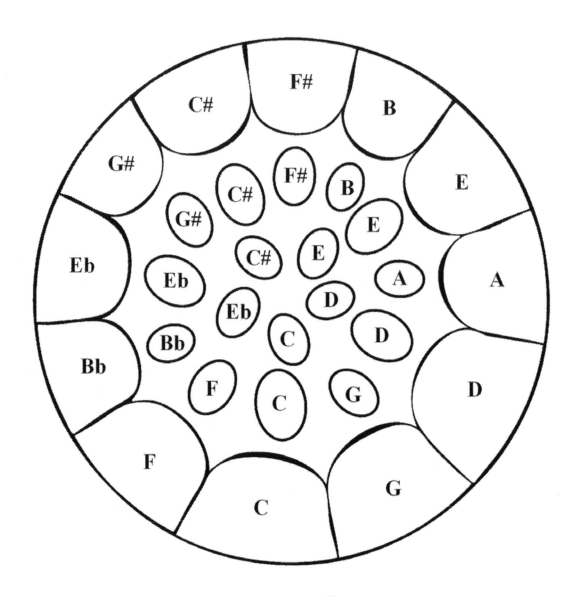

Circle of fifths Layout

Printed in Great Britain
by Amazon.co.uk, Ltd.,
Marston Gate.